I've Got It!

How many ways can people be creative?

page 23

Literature

Who 2
poem by Tim Seibles

**Sherlock Holmes and
the Red-Headed League** 4
drama retold by Lewy Olfson

How to Be a Great Actor 23
nonfiction by Staton Rubin

Related Readings and Projects

The Play's the Thing! 3
research project

How Do *You* Say It? 21
social studies connection

Lights! Camera! Color! 22
science connection

Book Fair 30
drama

Reader Response 32
critical thinking

page 4

WHO

by Tim Seibles

(for the Lewitsky Dance Co.)

Who doesn't
want to dance
to be inside the body
not somewhere beside it
to feel the arms and legs
hot and clean in a clear lake of air
like fins, as though every limb
were a fish for a moment
free of the water out of the world—
the body, strange as a planet
reeling in its own soft sparkle

Who doesn't want to dance
to let the body go gracefully mad
to fall into the music as though
from a cliff—every muscle a feather
every three feathers a bird every bird
bald blind and falling
as though the fall itself were the dance
as if the music were a cushion of air
a wind holding you up as though
in motion the body is a leaf is a
new fabric better than feathers better than water

Who doesn't want to remember the feet
to wash them in music
to feel gravity's tireless kiss
bringing you back, pulling you in
as if there were only you and the earth
and music were the sea
and the body were a small ship with lungs
as its sails—as though breathing
were dancing and dancing were living
and living were enough. Who
doesn't want to dance?

The Play's the Thing!

How did drama begin? When the first hunters acted out their fierce hunt for food, they were using drama. Perhaps it looked something like the dance the poet describes in "Who."

People down through the ages have performed for one another. Drama is one of our most creative ways to express emotions.

What do you know about theater? Here's how you can learn more.

Gather Information

1. Get an overview by reading a survey of drama/theater in an encyclopedia.
2. List some of the different types of theater, such as story drama, No (Noh), Bunraku, Kabuki, melodrama, theater of the absurd, and musical comedy.
3. Choose any two of these dramatic forms and find out more about them. Think about these questions as you gather information: How did this type of drama start? What are its characteristics?
4. Gather drawings and other visual materials about the two dramatic forms.

Organize and Draw Conclusions

5. List the characteristics of both dramatic forms that you've selected. Then compare and contrast them. Analyze how each one developed over the years and influenced other forms of dramatic art. If possible, name famous playwrights and actors associated with these forms.

Write and Present

6. Decide how to present your findings. You might wish to make a booklet, a model, a bulletin-board display, or a table-top exhibit. In addition to your presentation, perform part of a play that represents one of the dramatic forms you researched. For instance, you might perform a scene from E.B. White's *Charlotte's Web* to demonstrate story drama, or you might make a mask to use in a brief Kabuki performance.

I've Got It!

Sherlock Holmes
and the Red-Headed League

Play by Lewy Olfson Based on the story by Arthur Conan Doyle

Characters
NARRATOR
SHERLOCK HOLMES
DR. WATSON
JABEZ WILSON
VINCENT SPAULDING
DUNCAN ROSS
LANDLORD

NARRATOR: Dr. Watson, opening the door of Sherlock Holmes's Baker Street rooms, finds Holmes seated beside a man with the reddest hair he has ever seen. . . .

HOLMES: Ah, Watson, you could not have come at a better time. Here is a gentleman I should like you to meet. Mr. Wilson, this is Dr. Watson, my partner and helper in many of my most successful cases, and I have no doubt that he will be of the utmost use to me in yours also. Watson, this is Mr. Jabez Wilson.

WATSON: How do you do, Mr. Wilson?

WILSON: I'm so glad to meet you, Dr. Watson.

HOLMES: Try the settee, Watson. You know, since in the past you have shown such extraordinary interest in everything that is outside the conventions and humdrum routine of everyday life, I'm sure you will particularly enjoy the details of this case.

WATSON: Ah, Holmes, you know your cases have been of the greatest interest to me. But what is this particular case about?

HOLMES: Mr. Wilson here has been good enough to call upon me this morning, and to begin a narrative which promises to be one of the most singular which I have listened to for some time. Perhaps, Mr. Wilson, you would be kind enough to begin your tale again because my friend, Dr. Watson, has not heard the beginning of the tale.

I've Got It!

WILSON: I shall be happy to do so, Mr. Holmes.

HOLMES: Can you find the advertisement you spoke of in that newspaper again?

WILSON: Yes, I have it now. Here it is. This is what began it all, Dr. Watson. Here. Just read it for yourself.

WATSON *(Reading aloud)*: "To the Red-Headed League. On account of the bequest of the late Ezekiah Hopkins, of Lebanon, Pennsylvania, U.S.A., there is now another vacancy open which entitles a member of the League to a salary of four pounds a week for purely nominal services. All red-headed men who are sound in body and mind, and above the age of twenty-one, are eligible. Apply in person on Monday, at eleven o'clock, to Duncan Ross, at the offices of the League, 7 Pope's Court, Fleet Street."

HOLMES: Curious, is it not?

WATSON: Well, what does it mean?

HOLMES: That is what we must find out. But before I ask Mr. Wilson to relate any more, I ask you, Watson, to note the paper and the date.

WATSON: It is the *Morning Chronicle* of April 27, 1890. Just two months ago.

HOLMES: Very good. Now, Mr. Wilson?

WILSON: It is just as I have been telling Mr. Sherlock Holmes. I have a small pawnbroker's business at Coburg Square. Of late years it has not done more than give me a bare living.

Holmes: Do you work in it alone?

Wilson: No, I have an assistant—though, to tell the truth, I should not be able to employ him if he did not agree to work for such low pay.

Holmes: What is his name?

Wilson: His name is Vincent Spaulding, and I should not wish a smarter assistant. He could earn better money elsewhere—but, if he's satisfied, I'm not the one to put ideas in his head. He has his faults, too. Never was such a fellow for photography. Snapping away with his camera, and then diving down into the cellar to develop his pictures. That is his main fault, but on the whole he's a good worker.

Watson: He is still with you, I presume, sir?

Wilson: Yes, he is. We live very quietly, the two of us—for I'm widowed, with no family—and we keep a roof over our heads and pay our debts if we do nothing more. The first thing that interrupted our dull and quiet lives was this advertisement. As a matter of fact, it was my assistant, Vincent Spaulding, himself, who called it to my attention.

Holmes: How was that?

Wilson: Vincent Spaulding came into the office just this day eight weeks ago with this very paper in his hand, and he said . . .

Spaulding *(A young, vigorous voice)*: Mr. Wilson, I wish that I were a red-headed man.

Wilson: Why should you wish that, Vincent?

Spaulding: Why, here's another vacancy in the Red-Headed League. It's worth quite a little fortune to any man who qualifies, and I understand they can never find enough men with hair of just the right shade. Why, if my hair would only change to the same color that your hair is, I could step into a nice fortune.

Wilson: I've never heard of it. What is it then?

Spaulding: I wonder that *you* don't know of it, for you're eligible yourself for one of the vacancies, what with your flaming red hair.

I've Got It! 7

Wilson: What are the vacancies worth?

Spaulding: Merely a couple of hundred pounds a year—but the work is slight, and wouldn't interfere with other occupations.

Wilson: Tell me about it. A couple of hundred a year would certainly come in handy.

Spaulding: As far as I can make out, the League was founded by an American millionaire who was very peculiar in his ways. He was himself of red hair, and wanted to make life easier for those who were like him. From all that I hear, it is splendid pay and very little to do.

Wilson: There would be millions of red-haired men that would apply.

Spaulding: Not so many as you might think. You see, it is confined to grown men, from London, which was the American's native city. And as for color, why, the man's hair must be bright, blazing, fiery red like yours. . . .

Wilson: "Bright, blazing, fiery red like yours." Yes, Mr. Holmes and Dr. Watson, those were the very words he used. You can readily see for yourselves that my hair is of a full, rich color, so I decided, upon Spaulding's urging, that I would have a try at it.

Holmes: What happened after that, Mr. Wilson?

Wilson: Well, sir, I went to the specified address at the appointed time, accompanied by my assistant, Spaulding. Let me say that I never hope to see a sight such as that again. From all corners of London had come every man who had a shade of red in his hair. I didn't think there were so many in the whole country as were brought together by that advertisement. Every shade of color, they were—straw, lemon, orange, brick, Irish-setter, liver, clay—but, as Spaulding pointed out, none was as bright as my own. Well, sir, we pushed and pulled and jammed our way forward, and finally found ourselves next in line at the office door.

Holmes: Your experience has been a most entertaining one, Wilson.

Watson: Indeed, yes! Pray continue your story!

Wilson: The office itself was a small one—nothing particular about it. Behind the desk sat a man whose hair was redder than mine—a Mr. Duncan Ross, he told me later. As we entered the office, he shut the door, and said . . .

Ross: Your name, sir?

Wilson: Mr. Jabez Wilson, and willing to fill a vacancy in the League.

Ross: You are admirably suited for it, Mr. Wilson. I cannot recall when I have seen a red head so fine. May I take hold of your hair, sir?

Wilson: Certainly, if you like.

Ross *(As if pulling)*: Ugh! Mph! No, it's yours all right. I'm sorry to have had to take this precaution, but we have twice been deceived by wigs, and once by dye.

Wilson: Oh, no, sir. My hair is my own.

Spaulding: Indeed it is, sir.

Ross: Well, then, Mr. Wilson. My name is Duncan Ross, and I am myself one of the pensioners upon the fund left by our noble benefactor. I am pleased to tell you that the position is yours. When shall you be able to enter upon your new duties?

Wilson: It is a little awkward, for I have a business already.

Spaulding: Never mind that, Mr. Wilson. I shall look after that for you.

Wilson: What would the hours be, Mr. Ross?

Ross: From ten to two.

Wilson: A pawnbroker's business—for that is my trade—is done mostly at night. So I suppose I can trust my shop to my assistant here. Yes, yes, Spaulding, you're a good man. Yes, ten to two would suit me very well. And the pay?

Ross: Four pounds a week.

Wilson: And the work?

Ross: The work is to copy out the *Encyclopaedia Britannica*. Don't ask me why: it is the terms of the will. You will provide your own pens, paper and ink, but we provide the table and chair. Also, you forfeit the position if you once leave the building during the hours of ten to two. Will you be ready tomorrow?

Wilson: Certainly.

Ross: Then goodbye, Mr. Jabez Wilson, and let me congratulate you once more on the important position which you have been fortunate enough to obtain. And welcome to the Red-Headed League . . .

Wilson: With those words, gentlemen, he bowed me and my assistant out of the room. I was, at the same time, both pleased and puzzled.

Watson: Pleased and puzzled? How so?

Wilson: Well, you see, Dr. Watson, I was pleased with my new source of income, but puzzled over why anyone should want me to copy out the encyclopedia. In fact, by nightfall I had almost convinced myself that it was all a great hoax.

Holmes: Did it prove to be a great hoax?

Wilson: On the contrary. The next day, when I reported for work, there was the encyclopedia laid open upon the table, the page at letter "A." Mr. Duncan Ross was there, and he started me off, then left. At two o'clock he returned, complimented me upon the amount that I had written, bade me good day, and locked the door of his office after me.

Holmes: How long did this procedure continue?

Wilson: This went on day after day, Mr. Holmes, and on Saturday, the manager came in and plunked down four golden sovereigns for my week's work. It was the same the next week, and the same the week after. Every morning I was there at ten, and every afternoon I left at two. Eight weeks passed away like this, and I had written about Abbots and Archery and Armour and Architecture and Attica, and hoped that with diligence I might get on to the B's before very long. It had cost me something for paper, but it was worth it. Then suddenly—

Watson: Yes?

Wilson: The whole business came to an end.

Holmes: To an end!

Wilson *(A bit puzzled)***:** Yes, sir. This very morning, I went to my work as usual at ten o'clock, but the door was shut and locked, with a little square of cardboard hammered onto the middle of the panel with a tack. Here it is, and you can read it for yourself.

Holmes: Hm, how curious.

Watson: What does it say, Holmes?

Holmes: "The Red-Headed League is dissolved. June 22, 1890."
(Watson laughs, and Holmes joins in.)

Wilson *(Indignantly)***:** I cannot see that there is anything very funny. If you can do nothing other than laugh at me, I can go elsewhere.

Holmes: Oh, no, no, I shouldn't miss your case for the world. But you must admit that it has a slightly comical side to it. Pray, what steps did you take when you found this card on the door?

Wilson: I was staggered, sir. I did not know what to do. Then I called at the landlord's, and asked if he could tell me what had become of the Red-Headed League. He looked at me, astonished, and said . . .

Landlord *(Puzzled)***:** Red-Headed League, you say? I never heard of such a body.

Wilson: Well, then, can you tell me what happened to Mr. Duncan Ross?

Landlord: What happened to whom?

Wilson: Duncan Ross.

Landlord: Ross? I know of no one of that name.

Wilson: Well, then, what happened to the gentleman who rented number four?

Landlord: Oh, you mean the red-headed man. His name was William Morris. He was a solicitor and was using my room as a temporary convenience until his new premises were ready. He moved out yesterday.

Wilson: Where could I find him, sir?

Landlord: He's at his new offices. Let me see; he did tell me the address. What was it now? Ah, yes. 17 King Edward Street, near St. Paul's. . . .

Holmes *(Muttering)*: 17 King Edward Street. I'll make a note of that, Mr. Wilson. It may help us.

Wilson: Well, I already checked there, but there was no one there of either the name of William Morris *or* Duncan Ross. It was a manufacturer of artificial knee-caps. Well, at that, I knew not what to do, so decided to take the advice of my assistant, Spaulding, who said simply to wait. But I got impatient, sir, and hearing that Sherlock Holmes was very clever at such things, I decided to come here for aid.

Holmes: And you did wisely, Mr. Wilson. From what you have said, I think it is possible that a far more serious issue may be at stake than might at first appear.

Wilson: The issue is quite serious enough at it is. I have lost four pounds a week!

Holmes: Mr. Watson and I will do our best to help you, Mr. Wilson. But first, a few questions. This assistant of yours who first called your attention to the advertisement—how long has he been with you?

Wilson: He'd been with me about a month at that time. He answered an advertisement that I placed in the paper.

Holmes: Was he the only applicant?

Wilson: No, I had a dozen.

Holmes: Why did you pick him?

Wilson: Because he was intelligent and handy, and would come at half wages, in fact.

Watson: What is he like, this Vincent Spaulding?

Wilson: Small, stout-built, very quick in his ways, no hair on is face—though he's not short of thirty. He has a white splash of acid upon his forehead.

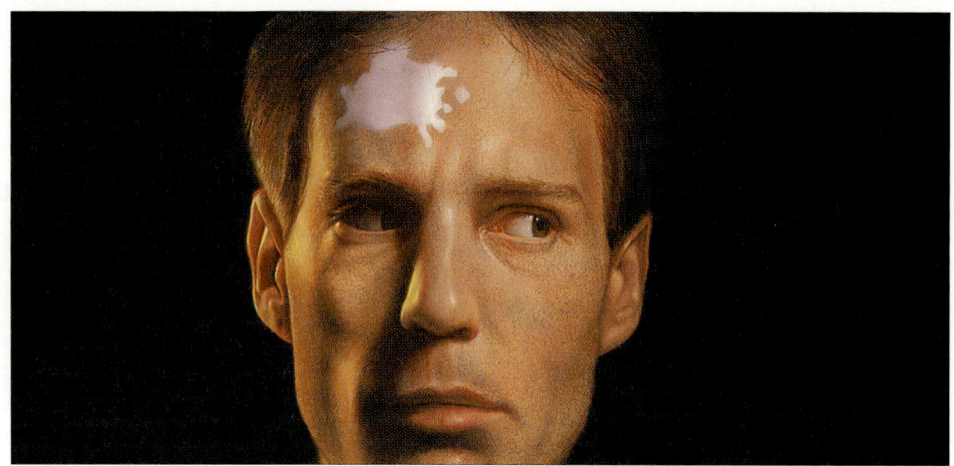

Holmes *(Excitedly)*: Acid, you say? Yes, I thought as much. Have you ever observed that his ears are pierced for earrings?

Wilson: Yes, sir. He told me that a gypsy had done it for him when he was a lad.

Holmes: Hm-m. He is still with you?

Wilson: Oh yes, sir; I have only just left him. But I must be on my way. Will there be anything else you require to ask of me, gentlemen?

Watson: Not for my part, Wilson.

Holmes: Yes, I have one more question. All the mornings that you were out—did your assistant attend to your business in your absence?

Wilson: Yes, sir, and he's honest and careful enough. Nothing to complain of, sir. There's never very much to do of a morning.

Holmes: I believe you have given us all the information we shall need, Mr. Wilson. I shall be happy to give you an opinion on the subject in the course of a day or two. Today is Saturday, and I hope that by Monday we may come to a conclusion. Good day, Mr. Wilson.

Wilson: Good day, Mr. Watson, Mr. Holmes.

Holmes *(After a pause)*: Watson, what do you make of it all?

Watson: I make nothing of it. It is a most mysterious business.

Holmes: As a rule, the more bizarre a thing is, the less mysterious it proves to be. But we must be prompt over this matter.

Watson: What are you going to do, then?

Holmes: We are going to the pawnbroker's shop of Mr. Jabez Wilson.

Watson: Whatever for?

Holmes: To investigate, my dear Watson. To investigate!

Narrator: Holmes and Watson set out at once for Jabez Wilson's shop. After leaving their cab a short distance away, they stroll down the street.

Holmes: There, Watson. See the three gilt balls? That is the place.

Watson: Yes, Wilson's name is painted over the door. But now that you are here, what are you going to do?

Holmes: First, an experiment.

Narrator: Holmes pounds his walking stick on the pavement.

Watson *(Taken aback)*: Pounding your stick on the pavement?

Holmes: And now, to knock on the door. I hope that Spaulding fellow answers.

Spaulding: Won't you step in, gentlemen?

Holmes: Thank you, but I only wished to ask you how one would go from here to the Strand.

Spaulding: Oh. Third right, fourth left, sir. Good day.

Holmes: Smart fellow, that. He is, in my judgment, the fourth smartest man in London, and for daring I am not sure that he has not a claim to be third. I have known something of him before.

Watson: Evidently Mr. Wilson's assistant counts for a good deal in this mystery of the Red-Headed League. I am sure that you inquired your way merely that you might see him.

Holmes: Not him. The knees of his trousers.

Watson: And what did you see?

Holmes: What I expected to see.

I've Got It! 15

Watson: Why did you beat the pavement before knocking on the door?

Holmes: My dear doctor, this is a time for observation, not for talk. We are spies in an enemy's country. We know something of this city square. Let us now explore the parts which lie behind it.

Narrator: Holmes and Watson continue on down the street and around the block. Holmes observes carefully each building they pass.

Holmes: Let me see. I should just like to remember the order of the houses here. There is the tobacconist's, the little newspaper shop, the Coburg branch of the City and Suburban Bank, the restaurant, and the carriage-builder's. That carries us right onto the other block, on which stands the pawnbroker's establishment of our friend, Jabez Wilson. This business of Wilson's is serious. A considerable crime is in contemplation. I have every reason to believe that we shall be in time to stop it. But today being Saturday rather complicates matters. I shall want your help tonight, Watson. Will you come to Baker Street at ten? Goodbye for now, then, Dr. Watson.

Narrator: Promptly at ten, Watson arrives at Baker Street, and he and Holmes take a carriage, and set off into the night. Watson questions Holmes about the adventure as the carriage drives them through the city. . . .

Watson: Will you not tell me, Holmes, where we are going, or whom we seek?

Holmes: I shall gladly do both. We are now going to the Coburg branch of the City and Suburban Bank. The man we seek is none other than John Clay.

16   I've Got It!

Watson: John Clay! You mean the thief and forger who has escaped the police so many times?

Holmes: The same, and you may add murderer to your list. His brain is as cunning as his fingers, and though we meet signs of him at every turn, we have never known where to meet the man.

Watson: Why, all of London has been on his trail for years!

Holmes: I hope that I may have the pleasure of introducing you to him tonight!

Narrator: Leaving the carriage some distance away, Holmes and Watson cautiously enter the bank with a key that Holmes produces without an explanation. They descend to the cellar. . . .

Holmes *(Softly)*: Here, Watson. Through here. Righto!

Watson *(Quietly)*: Is this the cellar of the bank, then?

Holmes: It is. We must act quickly, for time is of the essence. I perceive that the ceiling is thick enough. We are not vulnerable from above.

Watson: Nor from below. The floor seems . . . why dear me! A hollow sound!

Holmes: I must really ask you to be a little more quiet. Sit down on one of those boxes while I shade the light.

Watson: What is in these great packing-cases, Holmes?

Holmes: The 30,000 napoleons of French gold from the Bank of France.

Watson: What!

Holmes: It has become known that this gold was being stored, completely packed, in the cellar where we now find ourselves. The directors of the bank began to have misgivings about leaving so large a quantity of gold about, and now it appears that their fears were well justified. The bank is to be robbed tonight, if I am not mistaken.

Watson: How so? And only the two of us to stop the thieves?

Holmes: I have ordered an inspector and two officers to be at the one possible retreat—the front door.

I've Got It! 17

Watson: How, then, will the thieves enter?

Holmes: Through a hole in the floor.

Watson: What!

Holmes *(Whispering)*: Huddle in the shadows! One of the stones is moving! They are coming. Hush!

Narrator: There is a chink of stones, and then Vincent Spaulding's voice is heard faintly, talking to another . . .

Spaulding: It's all clear. Have you the chisel and the bags?

Holmes *(Suddenly)*: I have you John Clay!

Spaulding *(Calling out)*: Run, Archie! I'm caught!

Holmes: It's no use, John Clay. You have no chance at all. You did not reckon with Sherlock Holmes. It is no use!

Spaulding: So I see. I fancy my friend has escaped though. At least my struggle with you gave him that chance. You are not totally successful.

Watson: The door was guarded. There are three men waiting for him.

Spaulding: Oh, indeed. You seem to have done the thing completely. I must compliment you.

Holmes: And I you. Your red-headed idea was very clever.

Watson: Ah, Clay, you'll be seeing your friend soon—in court, you scoundrel!

Spaulding *(With dignity)*: I beg your pardon. You may not be aware that John Clay has royal blood in his veins. Have the goodness when you address me always to say "sir" and "please."

Holmes *(Laughing)*: As you wish, John Clay. Well, would you please, sir, march upstairs, sir, where we can please to get a cab, sir, to carry Your Highness to the police station—sir?

Narrator: A short time later, back at Baker Street, Holmes explains to Watson . . .

Holmes: It was obvious from the start that the purpose of the Red-Headed League was to get our friend, Jabez Wilson, out of the way for a few hours every day. The plot was suggested, I'm sure, by Wilson's own hair. The four pounds a week was a lure—and who could not afford four pounds who was gambling on thirty thousand? They put in the advertisement. One accomplice posed as Duncan Ross, the other insured that Wilson would apply. From the time I heard that the assistant had come for half wages, I knew he had some strange motive for securing the station.

Watson: How could you guess what the motive was?

Holmes: Wilson's business is very small. It must be, then, the house itself that was of value. When I thought of the assistant's fondness for photography and his vanishing constantly into the cellar, I realized at once that that was it.

Watson: Yes, I remember now. Wilson mentioned that.

HOLMES: The description of the assistant convinced me that it was the notorious Clay himself. But what could he be doing in the cellar of a pawn-broker, I asked myself. Why, digging a tunnel, of course, each day over a period of months. Then I wondered, what building could he be tunneling into? Our visit to the actual scene itself showed me that. Remember I observed that the bank was right around the corner from Wilson's?

WATSON: Now that you mention it, I do indeed.

HOLMES: I surprised you, I recall, by tapping my stick on the pavement. That was to determine whether the cellar extended to the front of the buildings. Then I paid a call on John Clay himself—at that time known to us as Spaulding, the assistant.

WATSON: Yes. You said you wanted to observe his knees. What did you see?

HOLMES: You yourself must have noticed how worn, wrinkled and stained they were—which was a natural consequence of his burrowing. All my conclusions assembled, I called Scotland Yard and the bank, and secured permission and a key for our admittance.

WATSON: How could you tell that they would make their attempt tonight?

HOLMES: When they closed their League offices, that was a sign that they cared no longer about Mr. Jabez Wilson's presence—in other words, that they had completed their tunnel. But it was essential that they should use it soon, as it might be discovered. Saturday would suit them best, as it would give them two days for their escape. For all these reasons I expected them to come tonight.

WATSON: Ah, you reasoned it out beautifully. It is so long a chain, and yet every link rings true. It was indeed remarkable, Sherlock Holmes. Remarkable.

HOLMES: On the contrary, it was elementary, my dear Watson. Elementary!

How Do You Say It?

The detective Sherlock Holmes was created by a British writer. You may think that English is English, whether it's spoken in America or Britain, right? Well, yes and no! Although American and British people have little difficulty communicating with each other, the two countries still have vocabularies of their own. Here are some words that British and American speakers use for the same things.

American English	British English
call (on the phone)	ring up
potato chips	crisps
diapers	nappies
elevator	lift
French-fried potatoes	chips
gasoline	petrol
hood (of a car)	bonnet
raincoat	mackintosh
sofa	settee
subway	tube
truck	lorry

Make a dictionary of the words that you and your friends use for everyday things. For example, you might use *rad*, *phat*, or *cool* instead of *wonderful*. Include at least 25 terms. Share your dictionary with some adults. Compare your terms to the terms they used when they were your age.

Lights! Camera! Color!

Lighting is a key part of scenic design because it affects the play's mood and atmosphere. For example, musicals are brightly lit to create a cheerful mood, whereas mysteries are dimly lit to create eerie shadows and a spine-tingling mood. Effective stage lighting is based on three qualities: intensity (brightness), distribution (area covered), and color.

The effects of combining light and color are amazing. See for yourself! Shine a flashlight through colored cellophane or crayon-coated plastic wrap to create colored lighting. What happens when you shine the colored light onto colored paper? Test the following combinations and complete the chart.

Lighting		Color observed
red light on red paper	=	red
red light on blue paper	=	purple
red light on green paper	=	
red light on yellow paper	=	
red light on purple paper	=	
blue light on blue paper	=	
blue light on green paper	=	
blue light on orange paper	=	
green light on green paper	=	
green light on red paper	=	
yellow light on blue paper	=	
yellow light on green paper	=	
yellow light on purple paper	=	

Study the results recorded on your chart. Think about different kinds of plays. What colored lighting would you use to create different moods? How do you think the colors of costumes and scenery affect the choice of lighting? Now imagine someone needs help creating lighting for a play. Write the ideas and advice you would give that person.

I've Got It!

HOW TO BE A GREAT ACTOR

by Staton Rabin

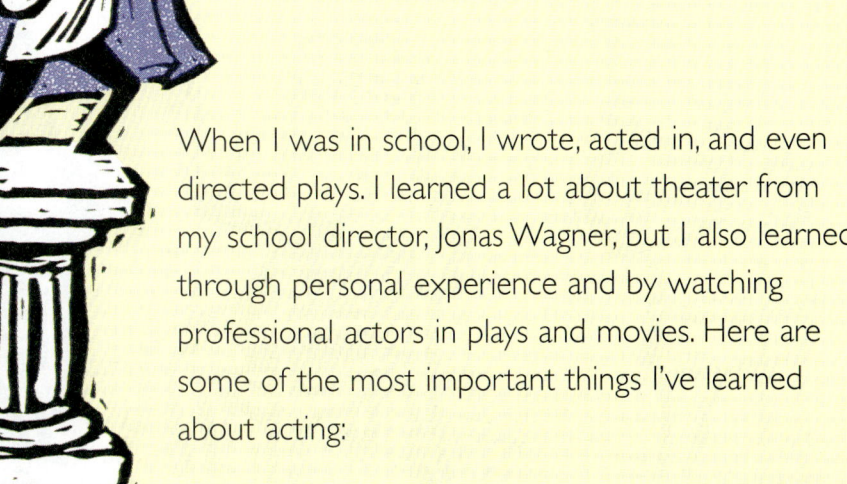

When I was in school, I wrote, acted in, and even directed plays. I learned a lot about theater from my school director, Jonas Wagner, but I also learned through personal experience and by watching professional actors in plays and movies. Here are some of the most important things I've learned about acting:

PICK UP CUES QUICKLY.

A "cue" is whatever comes right before your line. It's usually the last part of another actor's speech, but it can also be a sound—like a telephone ringing—or an action that cues (or tells) you that your line is next. Stay alert! Get ready to take a breath during the last word or two of your cue so you can say your line without having to pause first. Few things sound as professional onstage as an actor who is quick to pick up cues.

Be careful that you don't "step on" the lines of the actor who gives you your cue. That's not fair. But if you react like lightning, you'll be surprised at how much energy it adds to your performance. You'll pep up the other actors too, and make the audience sit up and take notice.

SAY YOUR LINES SLOWLY.

This may seem to contradict my first point. But it really doesn't. You don't want to pause *between* your cue and your line. But, please, take your time when you're speaking. Remember: the lines in a play aren't supposed to sound like words you've read and memorized. They're supposed to sound as though you just thought of the words yourself—right this moment. Real people *think* as they speak. So give yourself time to think about the words and what they really mean as you say your lines.

Of course, you don't want to say every line at a snail's pace. Experiment with when to slow down and when to speed up. Vary the volume of your voice. It can be very effective for a loud character to suddenly become quiet. Or for a mousy one to get loud. And really *listen* to the other actors' speeches—as if you had no idea of what they're going to say next. Many famous actors have said that good listening is the secret of good acting.

I've Got It! **25**

THINK OF THE OLD LADY IN ROW Z.

Our director used to tell us to pretend there was an old lady sitting way at the back of the theater. Mrs. McGillicuddy was hard of hearing, he said. So if you want to be heard, you'll have to speak up—or poor Mrs. McGillicuddy will miss the whole show!

Not speaking loudly or clearly enough is the most common problem for amateur actors. Learn how to *project your voice*, make it fill the theater by speaking from the diaphragm as opera singers do. Your drama teacher or acting books can help you learn how to do this. And remember to enunciate the words clearly. The audience will thank you for it—especially Mrs. McGillicuddy!

REMEMBER TO "CHEAT."

When you're speaking to another actor onstage, be sure to stand so that you're half turned toward the other actor and half turned toward the audience. Actors call this "cheating." If you don't cheat, the audience won't be able to see your face very well. And when you have to point or reach for a prop, use your "upstage" hand. That's the one that won't cross in front of you and block your face.

When onstage, try not to really look at or react to the audience. This can be a challenge, especially when they're laughing at your funny lines, and you're trying not to break up too! Just remember that you're supposed to be a real person interacting with the other characters onstage, not an actor playing directly to the audience—unless, of course, that's part of your role, like one of those old-time melodrama villains who cackles evil "asides" to the audience.

LEARN STAGE DIRECTIONS.

Sometimes these are written in the script, but the director is the one who usually decides when and where the actors should move during the play. These stage movements are called "blocking" and include directions such as "down right" or "up left." They tell the actors where to go as they say their lines. Blocking helps to keep the play moving along so it's interesting for the audience to watch.

If you know stage directions, you'll really seem like a pro. "Pick up the glass and cross down right, Miss Hossenfeffer. . . ." By the way, it may surprise you to know that "right" is the *left* side of the stage (and vice versa!) from where the audience is sitting. Stage directions are determined from the actors' viewpoint.

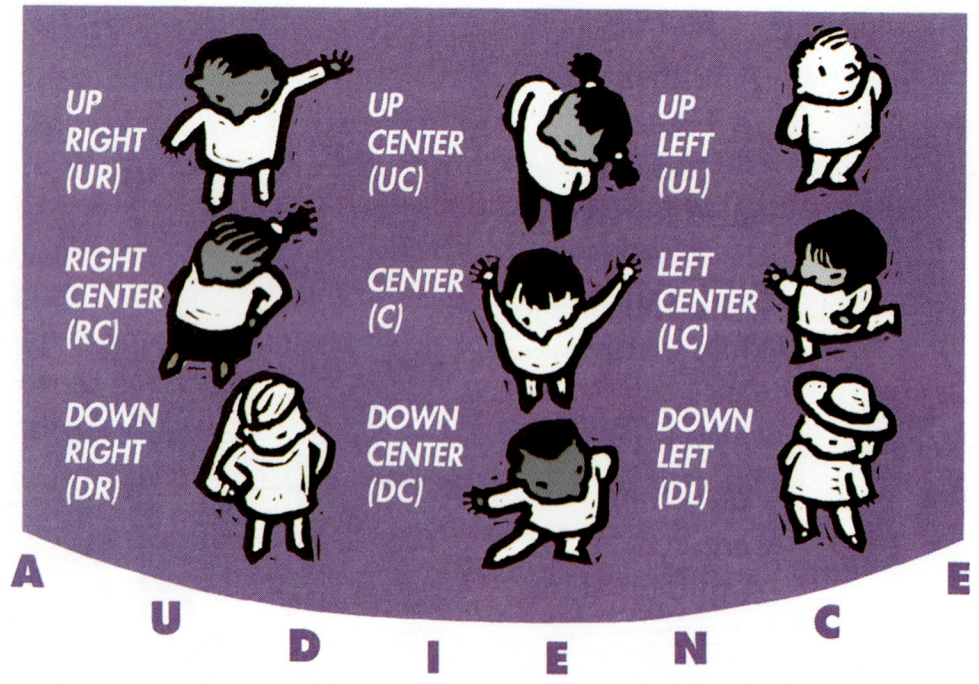

OOPS!

If you forget a line, don't panic. Say something. Anything! Except maybe "Oops! I forgot my line!" Try to think of what your character might say in the situation of the play. Then say it!

Congratulations! You're on your way to becoming a great actor. If you follow these simple rules, audiences should really enjoy watching you perform. See you at the Tony Awards!

I've Got It! **29**

Drama

A drama (or play) is a piece of literature written to be performed in front of an audience. The actors tell the story through their words and actions. Dramas can be read as well as acted.

When we describe a scene as *dramatic*, we mean it is exciting and memorable. The last scene in *Sherlock Holmes and the Red-Headed League* is dramatic because the mystery is explained. "How to Be a Great Actor" explains the techniques you can use to make your own stage performances dramatic.

Find Drama

Look for dramas in your classroom or school library. Here are three you might enjoy:

Blame It on the Wolf
by Douglas Love

The big, bad wolf defends himself in court.

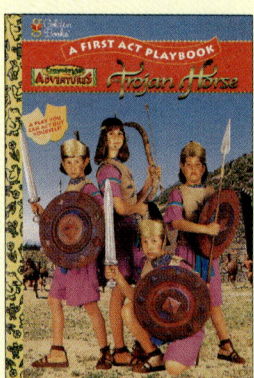

The Trojan Horse
by Keith Suranna

A humorous play about the Trojan War written for kids.

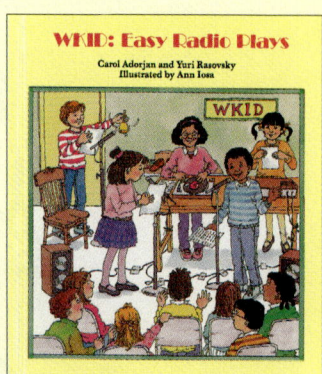

WKID: Easy Radio Plays
by Carol Adorjan and Yuri Rasovsky

A complete guide to producing radio plays. Includes scripts, radio terms, and tips.

Characters

Narrator
Sherlock Holmes
Dr. Watson
Jabez Wilson
Vincent Spaulding
Duncan Ross
Landlord

> **Cast of characters:** List of players

Narrator: Dr. Watson, opening the door of Sherlock Holmes's Baker Street rooms, finds Holmes seated beside a man with the reddest hair he has ever seen....

> In this play, the **narrator** tells you the **setting,** the location where the play takes place, and tells what the actors are doing.

Holmes: Ah, Watson, you could not have come at a better time. Here is a gentleman I should like you to meet. Mr. Wilson, this is Dr. Watson, my partner and helper in many of my most successful cases, and I have no doubt that he will be of the utmost use to me in yours also. Watson, this is Mr. Jabez Wilson.

Watson: How do you do, Mr. Wilson?

> **Dialogue:** The words that actors say

—from *Sherlock Holmes and the Red-Headed League*

Read and Think

As you read "Who," and *Sherlock Holmes and the Red-Headed League,* did you notice how the story was told through words and actions? Try to visualize how each story would unfold on the stage.

Share

Use what you learned from "How to Be a Great Actor" to perform a brief scene from a play. Remember, the word *drama* comes from an ancient Greek word meaning "to do" or "to act." Doing—acting, designing, directing—is what drama and theater are all about.

I've Got It!

Reader Response

1. Think About the Theme
How many ways can people be creative? How can the literature in this unit help you to use your creativity? Think about how Sherlock Holmes solves the mystery in *Sherlock Holmes and the Red-Headed League.* Consider what you learned about acting from "How to Be a Great Actor." Then explain why creativity is so important.

2. Ask a Question
Who is your favorite actor? If you could interview that person, what questions would you ask him or her about acting? What advice do you think you might get? Jot down the questions and possible answers.

3. Use New Vocabulary
What new words did you learn from these readings? List some new words you think you would use. Then write a few lines of play dialogue between two characters using these words.

4. Make Connections
"How to Be a Great Actor" gives practical, hands-on advice to performers. Which parts of this article would you teach to the actors in *Sherlock Holmes and the Red-Headed League?* How do you think it would affect their performance?

5. Analyze
Sherlock Holmes analyzed clues to solve the mystery. List the most important clues he discovered. Then explain how he used each clue to figure out what "The Red-Headed League" really represented.